MARRIAGE GOD'S IDEA
How to Make it Last...

Mario C. Alleckna

MARRIAGE GOD'S IDEA How to Make it Last...
Copyright © 2020 by Mario C. Alleckna

Cover design and additional photos
by Jeremy Giesbrecht
Photos by Cortney Adams

Contact e-mail: mcaall4j@shaw.ca

All scripture quotations are from the King James
Version of the Bible in the public domain.

All rights reserved. No part of this publication
may be reproduced, distributed, or transmitted
in any form or by any means, including
photocopying, recording, or other electronic
or mechanical methods, without the prior
written permission of the author, except in the
case of brief quotations embodied in critical
reviews and certain other non-commercial
uses permitted by copyright law.

Tellwell Talent
www.tellwell.ca

ISBN
978-0-2288-2453-4 (Paperback)

TABLE OF CONTENTS

Acknowledgements vii
Introduction
Divorce among Christian couples – A sad reality.................... 1
Part 1 Looking at the Foundation 7
Part 2 The Power of Words 33
Part 3 A Labour of Love 39
Part 4 Practically… 49
Part 5 In a nutshell... 64
A grandmother's words of wisdom............................. 69
Always Look to Jesus 71
Who is Jesus Christ?... 73
How to get to Heaven… 77
Other publications by Mario Alleckna: 81

Dedication

This little book is dedicated to my amazing children. May you pursue and find the special ingredients that make a relationship sweet and rich and a marriage the place of love and growth God intended for it to be.

ACKNOWLEDGEMENTS

Thank You to the One who came up with the idea of marriage, and who promises that ***"all things are possible"*** through and with Jesus Christ **(Mark 9:23; Matthew 19:26).**

And to my wife for being a true friend - always.

INTRODUCTION
Divorce among Christian couples – A sad reality

In the Bible's book of Proverbs, we are told that **"Whoso findeth a wife findeth a good thing" (Proverbs 18:22).** I imagine the same is true for both sides of course. However, when we look at the number of divorce cases among North American Christian couples, we might wonder why such a "good thing" so often ends up being the cause of some major disappointments and heart-ache? Hardly a day goes by without someone telling me about a Christian couple's separation or divorce. What a sad reality!

As a marriage breakup survivor, I am well acquainted with the hurtful emotions such a breakup brings with it. And I found out, just as in a war, there are no winners in the end. Everyone involved gets hurt in some way or another.

Although my first wife and I were not believers when we entered the commitment to be faithfully joined together, the rules for developing a lasting relationship are universal and therefore apply to none-believers just as much as believers. The bottom line is that God himself is the Author of the institution of marriage, and His intentions and rules for relationships and right living are valid for everyone.

The Lord God said, "It is not good that the man should be alone. I will make him an help meet for him" (Genesis 2:18).

A Beautiful Creation

"Who can find a virtuous woman? for her price is far above rubies" (Proverbs 31:10).

The Church – God's people

Interestingly, not only was it God's idea, marriage also has a very special place in God's plan for the Church. In His Word the Lord compares His relationship with the Christian Church to a marriage union, with Jesus Christ as the Groom and the Church as "the bride of Christ". We could say that our earthly marriage foreshadows the coming marriage between Christ and His Church, which obviously is not a building!

"Let us be glad and rejoice and give honour to him: for the marriage of the Lamb (Jesus) is come, and his wife (the Church) hath made herself ready" (Revelation 19:7; Ephesians 5:25).

One thing that many couples who are at the dating stage do not realize and fully understand is that there is a tremendous difference between dating and being married. Our God is a God of covenants. When He makes a covenant with people we can trust that He will never break it! He expects the same from us when we say our wedding vows, which means making a covenant to be faithfully joined together for life.

In other words, the change from just dating to being married comes with a great deal of responsibility and an unwavering commitment. For husbands this means to stop looking at other women with lustful eyes. For wives it means to show respect to their husbands.

"But I say unto you, that whosoever looketh on a woman to lust after her hath committed adultery with her already in his heart" (Matthew 5:28). "The wife see that she reverence her husband" (Ephesians 5:33).

A covenant relationship like a marriage, when built on God's values and standards, will always have His blessings.

Whether you are dating, married, or divorced and wanting to re-marry, the following thoughts are intended to give some basic, fundamental insights into what it takes to make a marriage last a lifetime.

PART ONE
Looking at the Foundation

"All Scripture is breathed out by God and profitable for teaching, for reproof, for correction, and for training in righteousness" (2 Timothy 3:16). "For by him all things were created, in heaven and on earth, visible and invisible, whether thrones or dominions or rulers or authorities—all things were created through him and for him. And he is before all things, and in him all things hold together" (Colossians 1:16,17).

"And every one that hears these words of mine, and does them not, shall be likened unto a foolish man, which built his house upon the sand" (Matthew 7:27).

Marriage is God's idea, and a truly great and lasting marriage must have a strong, immovable foundation of "God first"! The best and most effective implementation of the "God first" foundation should in fact happen as a way of life before marriage. If we make God number one, and if we seek Him first in everything, He might just add a perfect soulmate to our life.

"But seek first the kingdom of God, and His righteousness; and all these things shall be added unto you" (Matthew 6:33).

God first

"God first," *because* "God IS love"
(1John 4:8).
and "Love never fails" (1Cor. 13:8).

Nothing without the Holy Spirit

God gave us His Word to study and use as a manual for living, and He also sent us a Helper, the Holy Spirit, to teach, guide and protect us.

"But the Comforter, which is the Holy Ghost, whom the Father will send in my name, he shall teach you all things" (John 14:26). "And I will ask the Father, and he will give you another advocate to help you and be with you forever— the Spirit of truth. The world cannot accept him, because it neither sees him nor knows him. But you know him, for he lives with you and will be in you" (Jn.14:16).

"The person without the Spirit does not accept the things that come from the Spirit of God but considers them foolishness, and cannot understand them because they are discerned only through the Spirit" (1Cor.2:14).

The Bible says that the Holy Spirit is actually God. In **1 John 5:7** we read: **"For there are three that bear record in heaven, the Father, the Word, which refers to Jesus Christ...("the Word**

became flesh and dwelt among us." John1:14), and the Holy Spirit, and these three are one."

We can understand this if we look at water. Water is one thing, but it comes in three forms: Mostly as liquid; then as gas in the form of steam, and also as a solid, which is ice. Since these three, God, Jesus and the Holy Spirit are One, all of them are God. Instead of being a force, the Holy Spirit is a divine Person. **(Acts 5:3,4)**

In this verse Peter confronts Ananias as to why he lied to the Holy Spirit and tells him that he had **"not lied to men but to God."** Here we can see that lying to the Holy Spirit is lying to God. There are many more Scriptures showing that the Holy Spirit is a Person, even with emotions. **Ephesians 4 verse 30** tells us not to grieve the Holy Spirit. The Holy Spirit is God, the third Person of the Trinity, whom Jesus sent as a Comforter and Counsellor, and as the Helper who empowers us to live the life God calls us to live. **(John 14:16,26; 15:26)**

We could say that it took God to create us, it took Jesus to save us, and it takes the Holy Spirit to guide and empower us to live the life He has in store for us.

And how does the Holy Spirit guide us? Does He simply come and take over our lives? It all begins with a choice we must make: **"Choose you this day whom you will serve" (Joshua 24:15).** **"For we are labourers together with God" (1 Corinthians 3:9).**

Worldliness

"The world is passing away, and also its lusts; but the one who does the will of God lives forever" (1 John 2:17). "Choose you this day..." (Joshua 24:15).

Honestly...

If we truly believe in God, we must understand that we cannot be "wishy-washy" or lukewarm about following and serving Him. After all: He is the almighty King of the Universe who, one day, will judge the nations **(Revelation 3:14; Matthew 25:31).**

Unless we are ruled by God, His Holy Spirit, whom we receive when we make a true heart-commitment to Jesus Christ as our Saviour and Lord, we are ruled and guided by our flesh nature and or by the devil's influence. **"The Spirit gives life; the flesh profits nothing" (John 6:63). "And the great dragon was cast out, that old serpent, called the Devil, and Satan, which deceiveth the whole world: he was cast out into the earth, and his angels were cast out with him" (Revelation 12:9).**

If we want to benefit from the Holy Spirit's leading, we must make a clear and honest choice to follow Him daily. Recognizing and learning to hear His voice comes through spending time with Him. For example...

When we talk to someone on the phone for the very first time we don't right away know who's calling. However, after hearing that person's voice many times, we immediately recognize them.

The sooner we develop ears to hear Him by spending time reading God's Word and praying regularly, the better we are protected from making terrible mistakes and from being deceived. Trying to find the right partner for life is difficult as we are naturally attracted to someone's looks and how we feel about a person. God, on the other hand, is able to look into a person's heart, and what they will actually be like in a close longterm relationship with its daily tasks and trials.

"The Lord sees not as man sees; for man looks on the outward appearance, but the Lord looks on the heart" (1Samuel 16:7).

Jesus rebuked the Pharisees saying, **"this people draws near unto me with their mouth, and honour me with their lips; but their heart is far from me" (Isaiah 29:13; Matt.15:8).**

Here we can see that our relationship with Jesus Christ is a heart issue, not a head issue.

Behind the mask

"I, the LORD, search the heart, I test the mind, Even to give to each man according to his ways, According to the results of his deeds" (Jeremiah 17:10).

Compatibility

Once we have "fallen in love" it is as if our brains are put on hold and our feelings go into overdrive. It becomes very difficult to look at a person through the lens of cold, hard facts. Don't get me wrong, I am not suggesting looking for absolute perfection, after all, nobody is perfect! The question is: are two people perfect for each-other? Are they compatible?

You've probably heard it said that "opposites attract". Now, that may very well be true, but is that a good thing when thinking about marriage, or should we rather be careful not to fall for someone who is very different from us? (Let me assure you that the stuff you are able to overlook during the lovey-dovey phase of your dating relationship will not be so easy to put up with for the rest of your life.)

On a practical level: Although it seems to make sense that an outgoing and talkative person would do well in a relationship with someone who is quiet, introvert and a willing listener, always having to be the one taking the lead, over time, may feel like a lot of work.

The essence of being married is togetherness. Not just *being* together but also *doing* together. For a person who loves physical activities like fitness, working out and hiking, trying to find a mate at a book reading or arts club, where people's activities involve a lot of sitting, would not be very wise. Someone who loves adventure might want to travel and explore exotic places and try new foods. They might like to be creative and try different things, and are not afraid of venturing into the unknown. For such a person to be married to a couch-potato who always likes to play it safe and predictable might end up becoming a big frustration.

Am I suggesting that people with similar interests never argue? Certainly not! However, disagreeing over which type of Kayak to use for an adventure trip is much better than arguing whether or not you should pursue your favourite pastime in the first place.

The best way to finding a good match is in doing what you love doing. And although you might be attracted to someone who is the opposite of who you are, remember that it is the similarities, the same values and interests, that bind people together.

Compatible

Growing together on this sweet Journey of Life and Love with You – Just You.

Beware of Roadblocks

Thinking again about the emotional effects when it comes to dating and trying to find a soulmate, the feeling of being in love is like the icing on top of a cake–very sweet, but not much without the cake. Once we have "tied the knot," our marriage, much like our relationship with Jesus Christ, is a journey, not an arrival.

What began as infatuation, over time and with hearts slowly becoming one, should grow into a deep and true love for each-other. When Jesus Christ gave His life for our sins, it was love that motivated Him. In sacrificing Himself He taught us that love, first and foremost, is a choice, often inspite of how we feel. (I am sure we would agree that our Saviour didn't necessarily feel like being crucified.)

We can never build relationships just based on our feelings, as they are like the wind; subject to change, unstable and often unpredictable. And a house that does not have a strong foundation might collapse in a major storm. The same is true for our marriages. Unless our relationships are built on rock-solid ground, the first storm coming against us might cause at least some significant damage if not worse.

Watch for "Crocodiles"

If you are a Christ follower you obviously believe in the existence of a supreme God, but do you also believe that satan's influence is real? Because if you don't you leave yourself unprotected and vulnerable. And what about God's Word? Do you believe that it is true? To walk through life without paying close attention to the Creator and His instructions is foolish indeed. Here is what the Lord tells believers about the devil and how they must protect themselves: **"And the Devil was cast out into the earth, and his angels were cast out with him. And the dragon (satan) went to make war with those who have the testimony of Jesus Christ" (Revelation 12:9/17). "And the LORD said to Satan, "From where do you come?" "From going to and fro in the earth, and from walking up and down in it" (Job1:7). "Be sober, be vigilant; because your adversary the Devil, as a roaring lion, is seeking whom he may devour" (1Peter 5:8). "Lest Satan should**

get an advantage of us: for we are not ignorant of his devices" (2Cor.2:11).

God's Word is clear! If you don't want to get "eaten" by the devil, who has declared war on you, you must do the following: **"Wherefore put on the whole armour of God that you may withstand..." (Ephesians 6:13).**

And how does satan usually work? Aside from the fact that he has many helpers (one third of all the angels in Heaven came with him to earth **(Revelation 12:4; Job 1:7)**, in the book of Ezekiel **(Ez.28:12)** we read that he is full of wisdom. We can be sure that his schemes are very clever.

Just as God influences people to do good, satan uses people to steal and destroy. The flirtatious, new secretary at your office, who can't wait to go out for coffee with you, or the handsome instructor at your fitness class who seems so concerned about you, are the kind of people the devil might use to do his evil work. Although we shouldn't give satan too much credit, fearing him above his clear limitations, we also should never underestimate his power and influence. After all, he is the prince of this world **(John 12:31)**.

The strongest, protective foundation in life is a close, personal relationship with Jesus Christ under the guidance of His Holy Spirit. Naturally, such a relationship would also benefit our marriages.

There is one word that sums up why marriages fall apart: The word is selfishness. Self-fulfilment rather than self-denial is the message of today, even in many churches. We are told that God's love and grace, more than anything, means He wants us to be happy. In other words: 'If you are unhappily married, just move on. God understands, and He wants you to be happy.'

The idea of serving and putting others first, as Jesus taught, is not very popular in today's culture of self-focus. Of course, as Christians we should understand that self-focus is clearly not what the Lord intends for us. Instead, it is the focus on Him that will empower us to conquer the dragons that come our way.

We could say that Jesus is the glue that holds a marriage relationship together when the storms of life blow hard, and when temptation comes. And when we love our spouses according to Biblical standards **("as we love our self"; Ephesians 5)**, we have given our marriages the greatest chance to last a lifetime.

Those who are still trying to find that perfect mate should look for a friend rather than a husband or a wife—someone who shares the same values, hopes and dreams.

The Journey

Your hand in mine
together we walk
silently
no need for words
our hearts whispering
I love you

A wonderful friend can perhaps make a great spouse one day. But do not be "unequally yoked" by dating someone who is not a believer **(2 Corinthians 6:14).** Don't think that you might convert them over time. Chances are that they instead draw you away from God.

Remember what the Lord says in His Word, **"You shall know them by their fruits. Do men gather grapes of thorns, or figs of thistles? Even so every good tree bringeth forth good fruit; but a corrupt tree bringeth forth evil fruit. A good tree cannot bring forth evil fruit, neither can a corrupt tree bring forth good fruit. Wherefore by their fruits you shall know them"** (Matthew 7:16-20).

There will be visible signs, i.e. fruits, that a true follower of Jesus Christ produces and displays when the Holy Spirit is in control. When dating we should look for the fruit of the Holy Spirit in that person's life. **"The fruit of the Spirit is love, joy, peace, longsuffering, gentleness, goodness, faith, meekness, temperance"** (Galatians 5:22/23).

Once we are married we produce the fruit of the Holy Spirit together. Again, just as a marriage, the Christian life is a journey, not an arrival. Fruit grows over time, it doesn't appear instantly. And the closer we walk with Jesus, the faster we see positive changes and results.

PART TWO
The Power of Words

"Let there be light", God said, and so it was (Genesis 1:3). "Death and life are in the power of the tongue" (Proverbs 18.21).

Did you know that one of the main reasons why people struggle in relationships is a lack of meaningful, open and honest communication? According to a recent study, married couples, after only three years of marriage, talk for an average of only a few minutes during the course of a day. As a result, assumptions rather than verified facts often determine a person's feelings. Let's look at some examples of how not talking, negatively affects a marriage relationship.

When a spouse feels neglected and does not share her feelings, over time, resentment will build up and she might be drawn to someone (a neighbour; a family friend, the fitness instructor...) who seems understanding and able to meet her need for affection.

Then there is the husband who can't do anything right, and whose wife doesn't show much respect towards him. Instead of openly communicating how he feels, he becomes bitter towards her. The co-worker who shows her appreciation for him, slowly, becomes more and more attractive.

The fact is, some issues are not easy to talk about and often will be avoided altogether. Would you ever consider talking with your spouse about what it would be like to get a divorce? "Of course not!" you might say. "For Christians divorce is just not an option."

Interestingly, almost all divorced Christian couples never thought of, let alone openly talked about, divorce and how to avoid it. The idea is that it could never happen to us; or, by thinking or even talking about it, you are inviting it to happen. But isn't that like saying: when you talk about the risk and danger of developing heart-disease, you are sure to get it? The opposite is true! By being aware and talking about a possible problem before it arises, we can implement preventative measures. In the case of physical illness, this could mean planning to eat healthy and to exercise regularly.

Knowing eachother

When it comes to the prevention of a breakup in marriage, we must be aware of what each other's needs and desires are by openly talking about them. We shouldn't assume that a spouse should instinctively know what the other might need. Also: using hurtful, angry language instead of always respecting each-other as God's creation, only leads to resentment rather than openness to change or to find compromise. Something else to consider is that certain outside influences and "voices" can impact our lives, including our marriages. We live in a fast-paced time of constant changes. Today's markets regularly offer new things for us to buy, even when the old is not old at all and still in good condition.

Unless you have the latest and newest gadget, you couldn't possibly be content. The advertising media has done a great job, conditioning people's minds in that way. Such a mind-set, subconsciously, can also influence us as we look at our partners. When things have been rough for quite some time, unhealthy thoughts might enter a person's mind. Thoughts like, "wouldn't it be nice to be in a fresh, new relationship with that fresh, lovey-dovey romantic excitement just like the fresh interior smell of a new car?"

However, should you decide to drive your car for a very long time, how do you keep it looking and smelling nice for many years to come? Simply by working at it! The same is true for your marriage.

Togetherness

*Love never shared
is like a beautiful symphony
never played
a beautiful song
never sung*

PART THREE
A Labour of Love

"**What doth it profit, my brethren, though a man says he has faith, and have not works? Even so-faith, if it hath not works, is dead, being alone" (James 2:14/17)**

Walking by faith and trusting the Lord with every aspect, and in every area of our lives, is absolutely vital. But the fact is God wants us to do our part, **"For we are labourers together with God." (1 Corinthians 3:9). "Thus also faith by itself, if it does not have works, is dead." (James 2:17).**

When it comes to our relationships we must be deliberate in our effort to keep things fresh and exciting. Always just saying "I love you" without showing any tangible signs to prove it, is like making a promise and never following through. "But I work hard to put food on the table and enable us to pay the bills," a husband might say. "Isn't that enough to show that I love her?" No, it is not! Going to work or fixing things around the house have nothing to do with being married. You are just doing what you would do if you were single or perhaps sharing a place with some friends. The one thing that makes a marriage magically different from any other relationships is intimacy–a physical and emotional closeness that is only experienced with a spouse.

"...and the two shall become one flesh' so then they are no longer two, but one flesh" (Mark10:8). For us to show that we love our spouses we must be intentional, aiming specific signs of appreciation and romantic notions towards them. Just ask yourself what you did when you were first dating? Did you make sure you looked nice? Now, that you've perhaps been married for some time, are you still making a point of 'cleaning up' and smelling nice for the one you love? What else did you do to make yourself attractive or handsome? Did you buy gifts or exchange little love-notes? Did you make time for romantic dinners and getaways? Never forget what it felt like when you first fell in love, when you realized that "this is the one".

The one

Your gentle smile
softly touches my face
Your eyes
speak more than words
Two hearts
slowly becoming one

Cherish eachother

With the obvious attack by the devil on Christian marriages it is just not good enough to live together in the same place in some kind of a working relationship where romantic advances and passionate kisses have become rare luxuries. (The once a year flowers, and the twice a year help with doing dishes, obviously won't do much either.) Sadly, many couples would agree that, "if you're looking for romance, don't bother looking at home". And while husbands and wives are starving for affection, they are living side-by-side like roommates.

With the fire of being in love long gone they have become easy targets for someone to come in and ignite the sweet feelings of romance.

Aside from, first and foremost, building a strong spiritual foundation where we are guided and protected by the Holy Spirit, we must continually cherish our spouses in tangible ways in order to create a strong foundation for a lasting marriage. A good way to start is by finding out how the opposite sex generally works. For example: Women's needs are often quite different from those of men. They usually have a deep desire to talk and for someone to listen to them.

Good listener

"Finally, brethren, whatsoever things are true, whatsoever things are honest, whatsoever things are just, whatsoever things are pure, whatsoever things are lovely, whatsoever things are of good report; if there be any virtue, and if there be any praise, think on these things" (Philippians 4:8).

When a man never spends time talking and attentively listening to his wife, he slowly becomes unattractive. On the other hand, a husband who spends time showing interest and listening to his wife, rather than always just listening to his favourite sports commentator, remains attractive to her.

Men obviously function quite differently, as they are visually stimulated and attracted. When a wife lets herself go outwardly, his eyes will easily wander to the many pretty girls out there. "But I don't look very attractive after having my kids. There is nothing I can do, so why bother?" a wife might say. It is true; there is only so much we can do to improve our outward appearance. Having children often takes its toll on a woman's body. I think most men do understand this. But not even trying to do the best we can, will give the impression of not caring. And it certainly also doesn't have a positive effect on a woman's self-image when she lets herself go. If she tries her best to look her best for herself and her husband, she does all she possibly can. What more can a man wish for? And, since a wife prefers to be married to a handsome looking man, for him to become a careless slob is not only unhealthy but also rather unattractive.

You are Beautiful

Both husband and wife have a need to know that they are still desirable in the eyes of their spouse, even after years of marriage. Especially women, with the signs of hard work and motherhood, forever etched into their skin, need to know that they are still attractive to their husbands.

For a loving husband his wife's outer and inner beauty, over time, melt together, creating a beauty that goes beyond just the outward. He will find it easy to express how he still finds her attractive and wants to be with her physically. For a loving wife, she will find ways to let her husband know how she appreciates him, and how she desires his affection for her.

In the popular song called "Yellow Taxi", the singer emphasizes that, 'you don't know what you've got till it's gone'. We should never take that which is dear to us for granted!

Actively working on your relationship with your spouse truly is a labour of love, which will only benefit your marriage and your family.

PART FOUR
Practically...

"**Let every one of you in particular so love his wife even as himself; and the wife see that she reverence her husband" (Ephesians 5:33).**

Most of the songs ever written are about the topic of love. To feel loved and to belong are the two greatest and deepest needs of a person. The Bible tells us that **"God is love" (1John 4:8).** To know Him enables us to know what it means to love. We could say that we were created by Love, for Love, to love.

So, protecting your marriage begins with the One whose idea it was in the first place–God. Make time to read His Word and pray together, asking the Lord to bless you, your spouse and your marriage. There is truth to the old saying, "Couples that pray together, stay together."

Don't ever stop celebrating the gift of a special friend and intimate companion God has given you in each-other. Make time to be together, just the two of you, the way you did when you first fell in love. And once you are perhaps blessed with children, spend some special time when the kids are in bed. Go for walks together. Order in some food or go for coffee or a romantic dinner occasionally if you can. Aside from romantic getaways, find projects you enjoy doing together, like painting or redecorating your bedroom. Or perhaps helping with a community event. Join a local gym or hiking club. Same interests and activities bind together, and they are memory builders. Be a team and have fun together.

"Let your fountain be blessed: and rejoice with the wife of your youth." (Proverbs 5:18)

Rejoice

*Love me
like you mean it
hold me
like you care
see me
with your heart*

Not just words

Be intentional, just as you would when preparing to watch your favourite hockey or football team with friends on the weekend, or planning to spend a day at the Mall or a Spa with your girlfriends. Simply make a point of setting your mind on being with your spouse in a romantic way.

Always begin your special time together with this question: "How are we doing?" Or perhaps more specific: "How do you feel about our love-life? Are you satisfied? How can we make it better?" Be honest and open about the answers. Remember that regular, open and honest communication keeps issues from growing into relationship eating monsters.

Researchers have found that the two most common reasons for divorce are problems related to sex or money. Again, the difference between living together like roommates or being joint in marriage is a unique physical and emotional intimacy. In the letter to the Corinthian church **(1 Cor. 7:4/5)** the writer advises couples not to abstain too long from coming together physically as it might open the door for the devil. Seeing how much we hear about sexual misconduct on the news these days, we would do well in taking the issue of sexuality serious.

An unusual lack of desire to be intimate with one's spouse can have emotional or medical reasons, which should be talked and prayed about, and perhaps also addressed with a professional counsellor or physician. However, not feeling the need to be physically intimate can simply also have to do with a specific season in life. For example: A woman who has young children constantly asking for her physical attention and affection, may not feel the desire to be physical with her spouse as often as she used to. A good hug and some cuddling on the couch, besides a listening ear, might be all she needs to feel loved.

On the other hand, a husband who is blessed with a good dose of testosterone, might feel the need to regularly show his love for his wife by wanting to be intimate with her. Understanding that God Himself created our sexuality we must recognize its special and important place in a marriage relationship.

In the Bible's Book of the **"Song of Solomon"**, we are given a very vibrant and sometimes explicit account of the wisest King's exciting and romantic love life. There can be no doubt that a healthy sex-life makes a marriage strong, vibrant, and protected.

Loving your spouse means serving and being concerned with her or his wellbeing, which should make it possible to find satisfying compromises in your sexual relationship. Always remember to be sensitive and not demanding in your conversations. Naturally the Bible, as the perfect manual for living, offers great advice...

"Love is patient, love is kind. It does not envy, it does not boast, it is not proud. It does not dishonour others, it is not self-seeking, it is not easily angered, it keeps no record of wrongs. Love does not delight in evil but rejoices with the truth. It always protects, always trusts, always hopes, always perseveres. Love never fails" (1Corinthians 13:4-8). "Serve one another humbly in love" (Galatians 5:13).

Serving each-other in love will guarantee a great deal of satisfaction for both sides in a marriage.

Serving

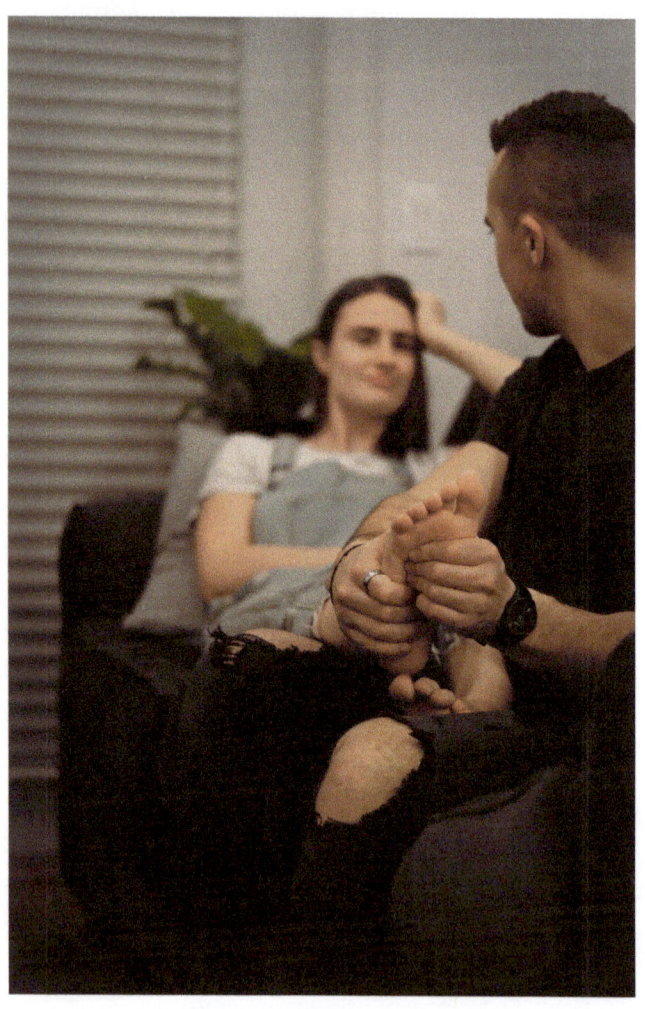

Let Me Be Your Servant

a hymn by Richard Gillard

Let me be your servant.
Let me be as Christ to you.

Pray that I might have the grace
to let you be my servant too.

We are pilgrims on a journey.
We are pilgrims on the road.

We are here to help each other
walk the mile and bear the load.

I will hold the Christ light for you
in the night time of your fear.

I will hold my hand out to you,
speak the peace you long to hear.

I will weep when you are weeping,
When you laugh I'll laugh with you.

I will share your joy and sorrow
till we've seen this journey through.

When we sing to God in heaven,
we will find such harmony:

Born of all we've known together
of Christ's love and agony.

Let me serve you,
let me be as Christ to you.

Pray that I might have the grace
to let you be my servant too.

Concerning your finances..., there are many services on the Internet who can help you budget according to your income. One advice I can give is that credit card debt will never magically evaporate. You will have to pay what you owe, and much more when you consider the interest rate you are being charged on top of what you owe.

And never depend on your paycheque when taking out a huge loan, which you plan on paying back over several years. No matter how secure your job looks today, next year might be a very different story! Now, I am not suggesting to never go to a bank and borrow some money.

After all, paying back a loan is one way to build a good credit rating. The issue is the size of what you owe. It is not worth losing a house over unpaid credit debt.

Many marriages have fallen apart because a partner lost their job, and the financial pressure caused severe stress in that marriage. It is always good to ask God for wisdom in our finances, and a wise person lives within their means!

"If any of you lacks wisdom, he should ask God, who gives generously to all without finding fault, and it will be given to him"

(James1:5). "Don't owe anyone anything" (Romans 13:8).

The good news is: With God it is never too late to get a fresh start, and to repair a mistake we might have made in the past. In fact, **"with God ALL things are possible" (Matthew19:26).**

Should you, or your spouse, have made a mistake, always remember this: One of the greatest weapons you can use to protect your marriage relationship is forgiveness.

Real strength of character

"And be kind one to another, tenderhearted, forgiving one another, even as God for Christ's sake has forgiven you" (Ephesians 4:32). Then Peter came to Jesus and asked, "Lord, how many times shall I forgive my brother or sister who sins against me? Up to seven times?" Jesus said unto him, "I say not unto you, Until seven times: but, Until seventy times seven" (Matthew18:21-23).

Jesus Christ forgave our sins, ALL our sins; how can we possibly not forgive! Unforgiveness is a terrible burden we should never want to carry.

Again, it is never too late to start fresh, no matter how difficult a situation has become. Too often we are drawn to focus on the problems we face, which might leave us hopeless, rather than on God.

When young shepherd, David, was facing Goliath, he did not focus on the giant's size and strength. Instead, as he had always done in the past when fighting a hungry wolf or lion, he focused on God's size and strength.

God is bigger

"And above all things have fervent love for one another, for "love will cover a multitude of sins" (1Peter 4:8).

Allow me to share a principle when it comes to our focus: Focus magnifies things. That, which we focus on in our lives, over time, grows bigger and bigger and becomes our motivation. If we constantly focus on our negative experiences in our marriage, our spouses' shortcomings, or our own mistakes, soon we are unable to see the positive or remember the good times.

Often, when a relationship hits rock-bottom, it is difficult to be objective and to see things clearly with emotions running high. Should you be going through a tough time, unable to see a way out, I suggest getting some professional help. An experienced counsellor can help you get past your hurts and show you ways to rekindle the lost fire of love. Your marriage is worth every effort to make it work.

PART FIVE
In a nutshell...

Be honest with yourself and see yourself as you truly are. You are not perfect. No one is! We are all born with an inherited sinful nature from Adam and Eve. It is basically in our blood to be sinners. You don't have to teach a young child to be selfish and aggressive, it comes quite naturally. And we were raised by imperfect parents in a very imperfect world where satan's spiritual influence is becoming increasingly obvious. **"And the LORD said unto Satan, Whence comest you? Then Satan answered the LORD, and said, from going to and fro in the earth, and from walking up and down in it" (Job 1:7). "The devil, as a roaring lion, walketh about, seeking whom he may devour" (1Peter 5:8).**

All of this has shaped us. Honestly ask yourself: Do you have a problem with anger? Are you hot-tampered, easily flying off the handle? Are you perhaps struggling with gossiping, jealousy or feeling ugly and inadequate? First of all: God didn't make any mistakes when He created you! You are **"fearfully and wonderfully made" (Psalm 139:14).**

Always remember that Jesus loves you so much that He even gave His life for you.

"For God so loved the world, that he gave his only begotten Son, that whosoever believeth in him should not perish, but have everlasting life" (John 3:16). "Greater love hath no man than this, that a man lay down his life for his friends" (John 15:13).

Ask God to help you change and grow into the person He wants you to become. He promises that **"all things are possible to him that believeth" (Mark 9:23).** Work on renewing your mind while asking Jesus to help you focus on Him and developing a positive attitude and mindset. **"Be transformed by the renewing of your mind" (Romans 12:2).**

And then, when you have found the one you can't see yourself without, make sure you pray together and read God's Word together. Ask the Holy Spirit to guide and protect eachother and your marriage. And pick your battles. Some are not worth fighting! I promise you that in fifty years you won't even remember what the fuss was all about. Make every effort to talk and work things out. Always be respectful and kind, treating eachother with dignity. Choose your words wisely. Listen carefully to each-other and hear with your heart. Try to put yourself into your spouse's shoes; try to see things from his or her perspective. Don't go to bed angry. It is worth staying up all night to talk and make peace.

"Let not the sun go down upon your wrath, and neither give place to the devil" (Ephesians 4:26/27).

Here is what I've read in an old medical book from 1944: "To close the day with a happy heart, and to find sleep and rest with a peaceful mind, these are two of the greatest blessings that help to maintain health and happiness."

Don't let crazy busyness wear you out. Make time for romance. Be intentional.

And remember, the closer you get to Jesus, the closer you get with eachother.

At the Cross

"With all lowliness and meekness, with longsuffering, forbearing one another in love"
(Ephesians 4:2).

A GRANDMOTHER'S WORDS OF WISDOM

Let me leave you with a short newspaper article I came across some time ago. Here you can find some timeless wisdom...

Dear Ann:

I found this letter pasted in the front of a Bible passed on to me by my grandmother. The letter was written by her grandmother when she married in 1886. I hope you will consider it worth printing.

"Dear Mary:

I look forward to your marriage and lovingly pass on this advice to you. Look not for perfection in your mate. You will not find it, and it's just as well. Living with a saint can be very tiresome. Let your love be stronger than your hate or anger. Learn the wisdom of compromise, for it is better to bend a little than to break. Believe the best rather than the worst. People have a way of living up–or down–to your opinion of them. Remember that true friendship is the basis for any lasting relationship. The person you choose to marry is deserving of the courtesies and kindnesses you bestow on your friends. And please hand this letter down to your children and your children's children. The more things change, the more they are the same.

Grandmother Jayne Wells,
Baltimore, MD., May 2, 1886"

Always Look to Jesus
by Mario C. Alleckna

**When life isn't fair,
and no one seems to care**

When friends are few and storms blow hard at you,

Look to Jesus

**When sorrow comes your way and
grief settles in to stay**

**When you feel down and low, and your
troubles only seem to grow,**

Look to Jesus

**When your past keeps haunting you
and you don't know what to do;**

**When your heart is heavy with guilt and
shame, and no medicine can ease the pain,**

Look to Jesus

**When times of hardship finally cease, and
newfound abundance brings you peace;**

**When winter has passed, and springtime appears
and there are only joyful tears, Look to Jesus**

**When the fragrance of love fills your
heart with new life from above;**

**When life feels right, and your sleep
is sweet and peaceful at night,**

Look to Jesus

When youth has slowly slipped away, and you realize we were not meant to stay;

When you feel tired and worn like some old clothes, broken and torn,

Just look to Jesus... Always look to Jesus

WHO IS JESUS CHRIST?

"**In the beginning was the Word, and the Word was with God, and the Word was God" (John 1:1). "The Word became flesh (Jesus Christ) and made his dwelling among us" (John 1:14). "He committed no sin, and no deceit was found in his mouth" (1Pet.2:22).**

Why was Jesus without sin, did He try extra hard to live a "clean" life?

"This is how the birth of Jesus the Messiah came about: His mother Mary was pledged to be married to Joseph, but before they came together, she was found to be pregnant through the Holy Spirit" (Matthew 1:18).

Allow me to explain:

All humans come from Adam and Eve. However, when Adam sinned against God in the Garden of

Eden an invisible sin-gene entered his blood. All people inherit this sin-gene. We could say that it is in our blood to be sinners. (You don't have to to teach little children how to be naughty, how to lie and be selfish.) Even a sinful thought condemns us! Jesus said that just to look at a woman with lust makes us a sinner, unfit for Heaven. No matter how hard we try to become good enough for Heaven it can never work because through Adam we inherited the sin-gene!

"...for all have sinned and fall short of the glory of God" (Romans 3:23).

Jesus Christ, however, was not conceived through a man who then would pass on the sin-gene to Him. Instead, Jesus was conceived by the Holy Spirit. Therefore, He was without sin!

"For just as through the disobedience of the one man (Adam) the many were made sinners, so also through the obedience of the one man (Jesus Christ) the many will be made righteous" (Romans 5:19).

Why do we need Jesus to get into Heaven?

Allow me to explain...

God decided that an offering had to be made for our sins, and He then would forgive our sins. God Himself made the first and the last sin-offering. After Adam had sinned in the Garden God Himself sacrificed a lamb and gave Adam and Eve the skin to cover themselves, i. e. to cover their sin. From then on God's people had to sacrifice animals for their sins. When God sent the Angel of death as one of the plagues to Egypt He requested that His people must smear the blood of a sacrificed lamb on the doorposts of their houses. Because of the lambs-blood the Angel of death passed over their houses and no one died. Jesus Christ is referred to as the perfect Lamb who was slain (crucified) for the sins of all mankind. And because He was perfect in all of His ways, without sin, He was God's last and final sacrifice for all of mankind. We are all sinners, but because of Jesus Christ, who was offered as a sacrifice for ALL our sins (past, present, future) we can all get into Heaven. **"For God so loved the world that he gave his one and** only Son, that whoever believes in him shall not perish but have eternal life" (John 3:16).

"God made him who had no sin to be sin for us, so that in him we might become the righteousness of God" (2Corinthians 5:21).

"Worthy is the Lamb (Jesus Christ), who was slain, to receive power and wealth and wisdom and strength and honour and glory and praise" (Revelation 5:12).

Our physical body will die one day, but our Soul lives forever! We can't save ourselves!

We must repent of our sins and choose to make Jesus Christ our Lord and Saviour today. He loved us so much that He gave His life so that we can be with Him,forever in His amazing Kingdom. In Heaven with Jesus there is no evil, no sickness or pain – just pure love and joy.

"Now repent of your sins and turn to God, so that your sins may be wiped away" (Acts 3:19).

HOW TO GET TO HEAVEN...

Jesus answered him, "Truly, truly, I say to you, unless one is born again he cannot see the kingdom of God" (John 3:3).

God created mankind to be with Him. However, when Adam and Eve sinned against God by eating from the forbidden fruit, they spiritually died and were sent away from His presence. For people to come back to God they must be born again spiritually. With honesty in our heart, accepting Jesus Christ as our Saviour and Lord, and believing in Him and His sacrifice on the Cross while repenting of our sins, gives us the new birth as we receive God's Holy Spirit as a seal of Salvation. **"In Christ you also trusted after you heard the word of truth, the Gospel of your salvation, in Whom also after you believed, you**

were sealed with that holy Spirit of promise" (Ephesians 1:13; 2 Corinthians 1:21/22). God cannot lie! He promises that ALL our sins can be forgiven because of what Jesus Christ has done on the cross. If you've never made a true commitment to Jesus, it is never too late... Just pray as you are.

Jesus paid the price...

*"You stand before God
as if you were Christ
because Christ stood before
God as if He were you."
– Charles H. Spurgeon –*

Please note:

There are many other great resources about marriage and the different aspects that make for a good, lasting love-relationship.

Regardless of whether you are dating or have been married for many years, I suggest that couples read the following Bible-based book: Intimacy Ignited: Conversations Couple to Couple by Dr. J.& L. Dillow and Dr. P. & L. Pintus

OTHER PUBLICATIONS BY MARIO ALLECKNA:

<u>Book:</u>
Awakening the Sleeping Giant –
The Church and the Road to Revival

<u>Music/Teaching:</u>
On the Internet: You Tube; Mario Alleckna;
"You are loved" (Music and text slides)
https://www.youtube.com/watch?v=Unl4jZTr4a8&list=PLzLC4h--rUnmgT89UEGtjfnbdy6NM_Sdi

<u>Teaching Blog:</u>
Biblical Truths – A Fresh Look
Wordpress Mario Alleckna

www.ingramcontent.com/pod-product-compliance
Lightning Source LLC
LaVergne TN
LVHW072023060526
838200LV00058B/4651